My United States

Connecticut

MICHAEL BURGAN

Children's Press®
An Imprint of Scholastic Inc.

Content Consultant

James Wolfinger, PhD, Associate Dean and Professor
College of Education, DePaul University, Chicago, Illinois

Library of Congress Cataloging-in-Publication Data
Names: Burgan, Michael, author.Title: Connecticut / by Michael Burgan.
Description: New York, NY : Children's Press, an imprint of Scholastic Inc., 2018. | Series: A true book | Includes bibliographical
    references and index.
Identifiers: LCCN 2017025783 | ISBN 9780531231623 (library binding) | ISBN 9780531247136 (pbk.)
Subjects: LCSH: Connecticut—Juvenile literature.
Classification: LCC F94.3 .B8715 2018 | DDC 974.6—dc23
LC record available at https://lccn.loc.gov/2017025783

Photographs ©: cover: National Geographic Creative/Alamy Images; back cover bottom: Brian Drouin/Getty Images; back
cover ribbon: AliceLiddelle/Getty Images; 3 left: Radharc Images/Alamy Images; 3 right: Jim McMahon; 4 right: Kerrick/
iStockphoto; 4 left: aristotoo/iStockphoto; 5 top: Aurora Photos/Alamy Images; 5 bottom: David Spates/Shutterstock; 7
top: George Ostertag/Alamy Images; 7 center top: Philip Scalia/Alamy Images; 7 center bottom: Randy Duchaine/Alamy
Images; 7 bottom: Cj Gunther/Epa/REX/Shutterstock; 8-9: Demetrio Carrasco/AWL Images; 11: Stan Tess/Alamy Images;
12: Jerry & Marcy Monkman/age fotostock; 13: Aurora Photos/Alamy Images; 14: Steve Dunwell/Getty Images; 15: Tier
und Naturfotografie/Superstock, Inc.; 16-17: SeanPavonePhoto/iStockphoto; 19: The Connecticut Post, Ned Gerard/AP
Images; 20: Tigatelu/Dreamstime; 22 left: grebeshkovmaxim/Shutterstock; 22 right: Flag Illustrations/Alamy Images;
23 center left: Sarin Images/The Granger Collection; 23 top left: nitsawan katerattanakul/Shutterstock; 23 bottom right:
David Spates/Shutterstock; 23 center right: Ziva_K/iStockphoto; 23 bottom left: Kerrick/iStockphoto; 23 top right: aris-
totoo/iStockphoto; 24-25: Evan Richman/The Boston Globe/Getty Images; 27: Marilyn Angel Wynn/The Image Works; 29:
North Wind Picture Archives; 30 bottom right: P.Spiro/Alamy Images; 30 top right: Chronicle/Alamy Images; 30 top left:
North Wind Picture Archives; 30 bottom left: Marilyn Angel Wynn/The Image Works; 31 top left: SeanPavonePhoto/iStock-
photo; 31 bottom: Aurora Photos/Alamy Images; 31 top right: PhotoQuest/Getty Images; 32: PhotoQuest/Getty Images;
33: Underwood Photo Archives/Superstock, Inc.; 34-35: Tony Cenicola/The New York Times/Redux; 36: Tim Clayton/
Corbis/Getty Images; 37: fotoguy22/iStockphoto; 38: Andre Jenny/Alamy Images; 39: Mike Segar/Reuters; 40 inset: bho-
fack2/iStockphoto; 40 bottom: PepitoPhotos/iStockphoto; 41: Steve Glass/Aurora Photos; 42 top: Photo Researchers/
Science Source; 42 center: North Wind Picture Archives/Alamy Images; 42 bottom left: North Wind Picture Archives/
Alamy Images; 42 bottom right: Heritage Images/Getty Images; 43 top left: Keystone-France/Getty Images; 43 center:
Pictorial Press Ltd/Alamy Images; 43 top right: Shaw/Everett Collection; 43 bottom left: Peter Hvizdak/The Image Works;
43 bottom center: Andia/Alamy Images; 43 bottom right: Science Source; 44 bottom left: AlexAlmighty/Shutterstock; 44
bottom left: British Library/The Image Works; 44 top: GL Archive/Alamy Images; 45 top right: Media Bakery; 45 top left:
photosync/Shutterstock; 45 center: Everett Collection/Superstock, Inc.; 45 bottom: Q-Images/Alamy Images.

Maps by Map Hero, Inc.

Front cover: A boat at Mystic Seaport

**Back cover: Plainville Fire Company
Hot Air Balloon Festival**

Welcome to Connecticut

Find the Truth!

Everything you are about to read is true *except* for one of the sentences on this page.

Which one is **TRUE**?

T or F Many U.S. Navy submarines are made in Connecticut.

T or F Connecticut is the third-largest state in the country.

Find the answers in this book.

UNITED STATES

Connecticut

Contents

THE BIG TRUTH!

Almandine
garnet

What Represents Connecticut?

Which designs, objects,
plants, and animals
symbolize Connecticut? **22**

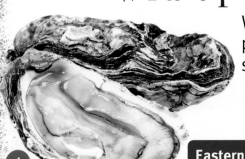

Eastern oyster

Huge waves during Superstorm Sandy

American robin

This Is Connecticut!

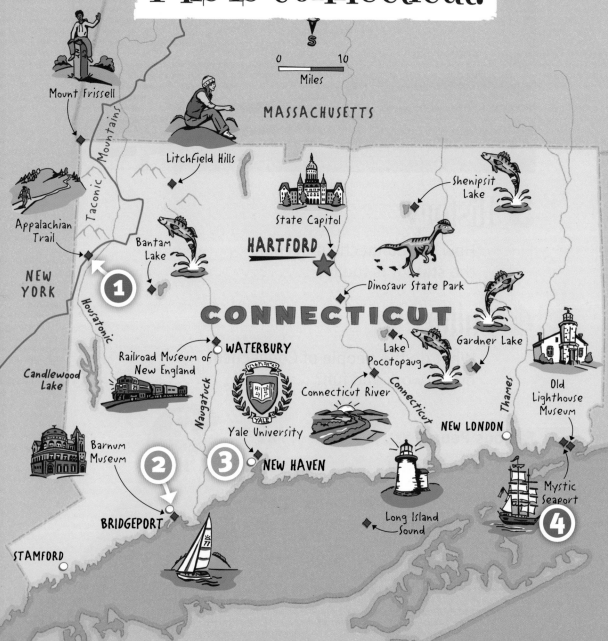

Mount Frissell

Litchfield Hills

MASSACHUSETTS

0   10
Miles

Appalachian Trail

Taconic Mountains

Shenipsit Lake

State Capitol

HARTFORD

Bantam Lake

Dinosaur State Park

NEW YORK

Housatonic

CONNECTICUT

Candlewood Lake

Railroad Museum of New England

WATERBURY

Naugatuck

Lake Pocotopaug

Gardner Lake

Connecticut River

Connecticut

Yale University

Thames

NEW LONDON

Old Lighthouse Museum

Barnum Museum

NEW HAVEN

BRIDGEPORT

STAMFORD

Long Island Sound

Mystic Seaport

① ② ③ ④

NEW YORK

ATLANTIC OCEAN

MASS

① Appalachian Trail

This famous hiking trail passes through northwestern Connecticut as part of a route that extends from Georgia to Maine. One of the world's longest hiking trails, it offers incredible views of Connecticut's natural landscape.

② Barnum Museum

RHODE ISLAND

This museum in Bridgeport was founded by P. T. Barnum, the legendary entertainer and businessman who helped start the famous Barnum and Bailey Circus. It displays artifacts from Barnum's life and the history of Bridgeport.

③ New Haven

One of Connecticut's oldest cities, New Haven is the home of the world-famous Yale University and several museums. The Peabody Museum features dinosaur bones.

④ Mystic Seaport

Visitors to Mystic Seaport explore what life was like in a 19th-century fishing village. Attractions include the *Charles W. Morgan*, the last wooden whaling ship in the world. It was built in the United States in 1841.

The word *Connecticut* comes from an Algonquian Indian word that means "long tidal river."

Land and Wildlife

As the third-smallest state in the country, Connecticut is not very big. However, it is packed with just about every kind of natural beauty you can imagine. Rolling hills line deep valleys. Forests fill almost every corner of the state. The shore offers people a chance to swim, fish, and sail. One of the six states that make up a region called New England, Connecticut is also where many of America's historic "firsts" took place.

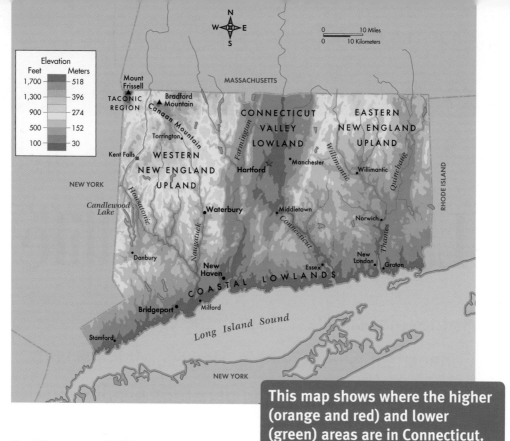

This map shows where the higher (orange and red) and lower (green) areas are in Connecticut.

Hills and Rivers

Connecticut has four major land areas. To the south, the state borders a body of water called Long Island Sound. The land along the shore is flat. The eastern and western halves of the state are marked by hills, with the highest ones found in the west. The state's highest point of 2,380 feet (725 meters) lies on the slope of Mount Frissell.

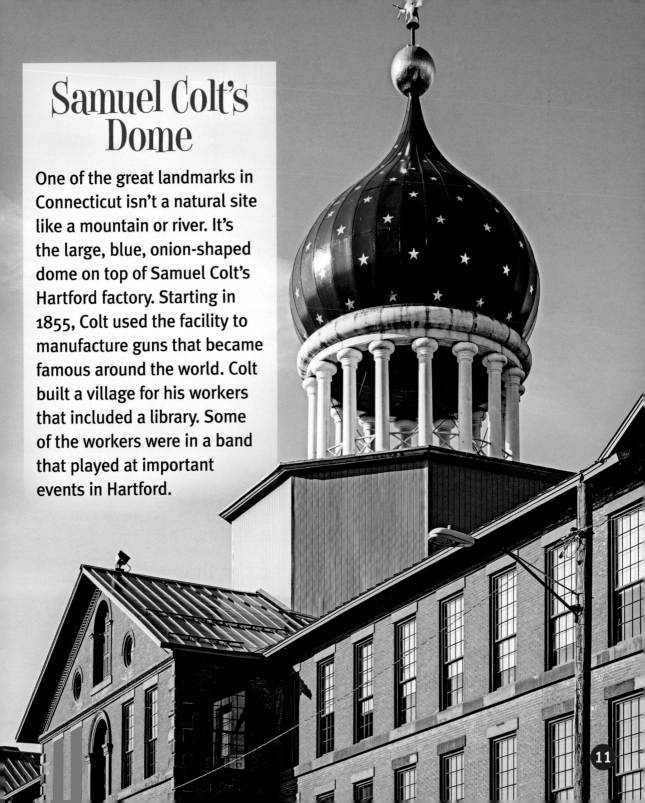

Samuel Colt's Dome

One of the great landmarks in Connecticut isn't a natural site like a mountain or river. It's the large, blue, onion-shaped dome on top of Samuel Colt's Hartford factory. Starting in 1855, Colt used the facility to manufacture guns that became famous around the world. Colt built a village for his workers that included a library. Some of the workers were in a band that played at important events in Hartford.

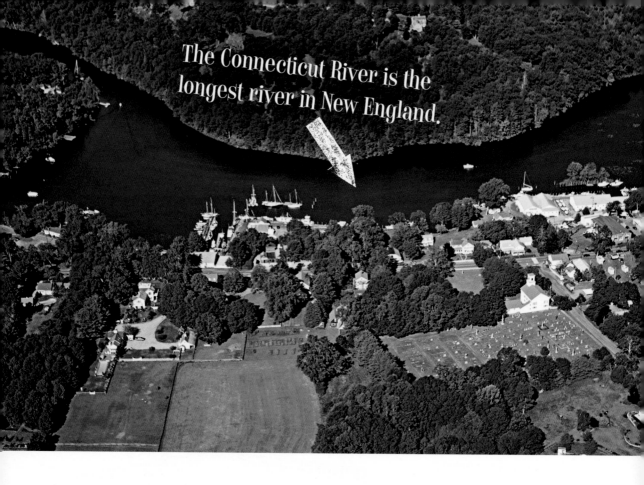

The Connecticut River is the longest river in New England.

In between the two hilly regions is a valley that is almost perfectly divided in half by the Connecticut River. **Silt** that collects at the mouth of the river prevented Connecticut's early residents from building a major port there. The state's other major river is the Housatonic, which flows through the western part of the state.

Climate

People who like to experience four distinct seasons will love Connecticut. Across the state, winters are snowy, and summers are warm. The shoreline tends to get a little less snow, and the western hills are the coldest part of the state. Summer temperatures average about 70 degrees Fahrenheit (21 degress Celsius). Hurricanes are a rarity. But in 2012 Superstorm Sandy, which had formerly been a hurricane, damaged several thousand homes in the state.

MAXIMUM TEMPERATURE
106°F

MINIMUM TEMPERATURE
-32°F

Huge waves were just one of the issues that faced Connecticut when Superstorm Sandy blew in.

A field of daffodils blooms in spring.

Many Kinds of Plants

Compared to many states, Connecticut has a lot of forests. They cover almost 60 percent of the state's land. Common trees include red maple, birch, beech, pine, and several types of oak. Connecticut's forests are also home to shrubs such as wild blueberries and the mountain laurel. Colorful wildflowers bloom around the state at different times of the year. Some of the most common include trilliums, lady's slipper, and elderberry.

Wildlife of All Sizes

Many different animal species dwell in Connecticut. They range in size from small squirrels and rabbits to enormous black bears and moose. Animals found along the state's rivers include otters and beavers. Dozens of bird species fly across the state. These include several types of owls and wild turkeys. Connecticut also has many turtles and salamanders in its swamps and marshes.

Peregrine falcons almost disappeared along the East Coast. In 1997, a pair nested on top of one of Hartford's tallest buildings, producing three chicks.

The dome of Connecticut's capitol is covered with a thin layer of gold.

CHAPTER 2

Government

In **colonial** times, Connecticut had two capital cities. The colony's lawmakers met in Hartford in May and in New Haven in October. This practice continued even after Connecticut became a state. But in 1873, the state decided to make Hartford its only capital, and work soon began on a new building where lawmakers could meet. The capitol opened in 1879 and is still used today.

Three Parts, One Government

Like the U.S. government, Connecticut has three branches of government. The legislative branch is called the General Assembly. It is divided into the House of Representatives and the Senate, and makes the state's laws. The executive branch, under the governor, carries out the laws. The judicial branch's courts enforce the laws.

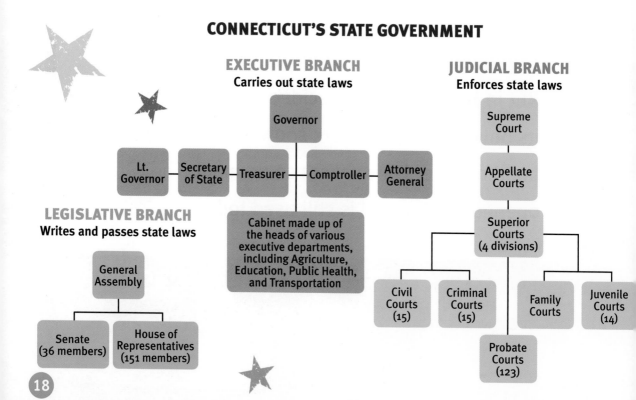

CONNECTICUT'S STATE GOVERNMENT

EXECUTIVE BRANCH
Carries out state laws

Governor

Lt. Governor — Secretary of State — Treasurer — Comptroller — Attorney General

Cabinet made up of the heads of various executive departments, including Agriculture, Education, Public Health, and Transportation

JUDICIAL BRANCH
Enforces state laws

Supreme Court

Appellate Courts

Superior Courts (4 divisions)

Civil Courts (15)

Criminal Courts (15)

Family Courts

Juvenile Courts (14)

Probate Courts (123)

LEGISLATIVE BRANCH
Writes and passes state laws

General Assembly

Senate (36 members)

House of Representatives (151 members)

A Love of Local Control

Unlike most states, Connecticut doesn't have county governments. Instead, officials in the state's 169 towns make and carry out local laws.

A Connecticut resident speaks up with a question during a town hall meeting with the governor in Bridgeport.

Some towns are also divided into smaller areas called boroughs that elect their own officials.

A traditional form of government in Connecticut is the town meeting. Voters usually meet once a year to discuss and then vote on important issues, such as how to spend tax money. Connecticut's people enjoy having the direct say in local government issues that these meetings offer.

19

Connecticut's National Role

Each state sends elected officials to represent it in the U.S. Congress. Like every state, Connecticut has two senators. The U.S. House of Representatives relies on a state's population to determine its numbers. Connecticut has five representatives in the House.

Every four years, states vote on the next U.S. president. Each state is granted a number of electoral votes based on its number of members in Congress.

2 senators and 5 representatives

7 electoral votes

With seven electoral votes, Connecticut's voice in presidential elections is below average compared to other states.

Representing Connecticut

Elected officials in Connecticut represent a population with a range of interests, lifestyles, and backgrounds.

Ethnicity (2015 estimates)

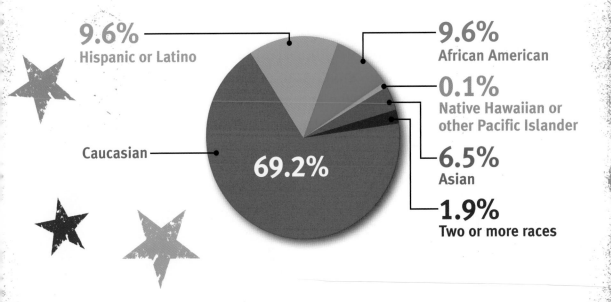

9.6%
Hispanic or Latino

9.6%
African American

0.1%
Native Hawaiian or other Pacific Islander

Caucasian

69.2%

6.5%
Asian

1.9%
Two or more races

67% own their own homes.

88% live in cities.

The state has **199,331** veterans.

14% of Connecticut residents were born in other countries.

90% of the population graduated from high school.

What Represents Connecticut?

States choose specific animals, plants, and objects to represent the values and characteristics of the land and its people. Find out why these symbols were chosen to represent Connecticut or discover surprising curiosities about them.

Seal

The three grapevines on Connecticut's state seal are thought to represent the colonies of Hartford, New Haven, and Saybrook, which united to create Connecticut. The banner under the vines has a Latin saying meaning, "He who transplanted still sustains." The words around the seal are also in Latin. They say, "Seal of the State of Connecticut."

Flag

Connecticut's flag borrows the grapevines and Latin phrase of the state seal. These images appear on a white shield set against a blue background.

Eastern Oyster

STATE SHELLFISH

This tasty shellfish has been a favorite food among Connecticut's residents since the arrival of the earliest Native Americans.

Mountain Laurel

STATE FLOWER

This beautiful flower grows on bushes that are common throughout Connecticut.

Praying Mantis

STATE INSECT

The praying mantis is not native to Connecticut, but is common there today.

Charter Oak

STATE TREE

According to legend, colonial leaders used this tree to hide an important document from a British official.

Almandine Garnet

STATE MINERAL

Connecticut is a leading supplier of this mineral. It is used to make blades and sandpaper.

American Robin

STATE BIRD

This bird spends winters in New England and is always a welcome sight for the people of Connecticut.

Pequots in Mashantucket continue to celebrate the harvest each year with a huge festival where they dress in traditional clothing.

1443

CHAPTER 3

History

Connecticut is known for producing inventors and thinkers who have helped improve life for all Americans. The state's earliest Native American residents created long paths through the woods that are now some of Connecticut's major roads. Later, after Connecticut became a state, many of its residents built things that helped transport people and goods—from some of the first bicycles to fast-flying helicopters.

The First Settlers

More than 10,000 years ago, a great sheet of ice covered Connecticut. As it melted, Native Americans from nearby areas began to move into the region. At first, they mostly hunted and fished for food. They also gathered wild berries and nuts. A little more than 1,000 years ago, people began to grow crops such as corn, squash, and beans. Farming led to the growth of larger, more permanent villages. People used wooden poles, bark, and animal skins to make dome-shaped homes called wigwams.

This map shows some of the major tribes that lived in what is now Connecticut before Europeans came.

Canoes were a common way for Pequots to travel by water.

The Native Americans of Connecticut spoke different forms of a language called Algonquian. Each group had its own version of this language. One of the largest groups was the Pequots. They lived in the southeastern part of the region. One of their special events was a clambake. Heated stones and seaweed created steam that was used to cook lobsters, clams, and corn. The remaining Pequots in the state still hold clambakes today.

Europeans Arrive

The Dutch were the first Europeans to sail up the Connecticut River. In 1633, they built a trading post near what is now Hartford. The same year, English **Puritans** from Massachusetts settled farther north along the river. Soon, more groups of Puritans followed, and Connecticut became an English colony.

Europeans brought diseases that killed many of the Native Americans. In 1637, the English settlers went to war with the Pequots. Hundreds of Pequots were killed, and some survivors were forced into slavery.

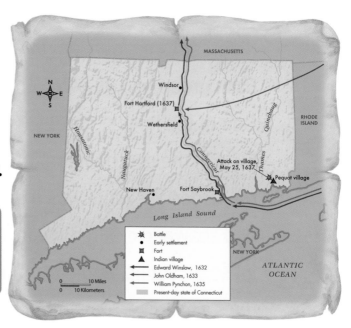

This map shows routes European explorers took as they explored and settled what is now Connecticut.

Land along the Connecticut and other rivers was valuable to farmers and merchants.

Farming was good along Connecticut's rivers. When farmers grew more than they needed, they sold their crops to other colonies. The goods were transported on ships built along the shores of the Connecticut River. Some residents became wealthy merchants and bought slaves from Africa. Some of the merchants also owned the ships that brought these slaves to the colonies. By 1774, about 5,000 African slaves lived in Connecticut, along with some free Africans.

Independence

Connecticut was one of the 13 British colonies in America that united in 1775 to fight for independence from Great Britain's rule. Connecticut men, both black and white, fought in the Revolutionary War. Connecticut also provided food and supplies for the troops. The American colonists won their independence in 1783, and Connecticut officially became a state in 1788.

Timeline of Connecticut Events

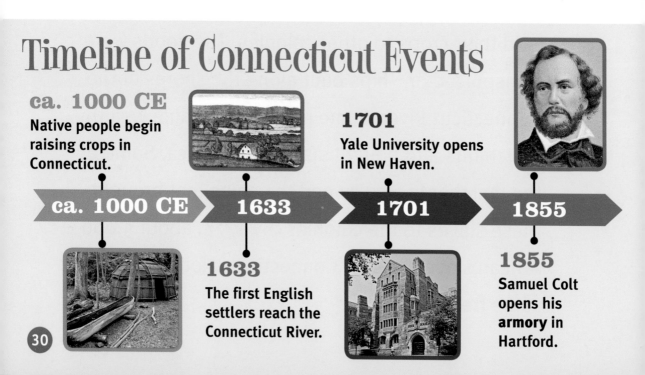

ca. 1000 CE
Native people begin raising crops in Connecticut.

1701
Yale University opens in New Haven.

ca. 1000 CE ▸ 1633 ▸ 1701 ▸ 1855

1633
The first English settlers reach the Connecticut River.

1855
Samuel Colt opens his armory in Hartford.

As the new country grew, Connecticut became a center for manufacturing. Eli Whitney, Samuel Colt, and others made guns. Several men set up businesses making clocks. Meanwhile, shipyards built ships used to hunt whales or carry goods around the world. Through the 1800s, **immigrants** came to Connecticut seeking jobs in the growing factories. Most came from Europe and Canada.

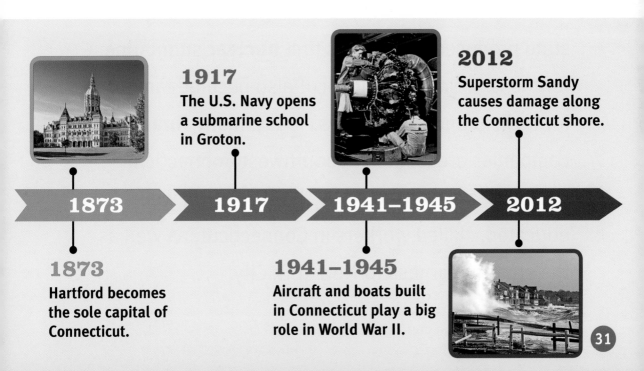

1917
The U.S. Navy opens a submarine school in Groton.

2012
Superstorm Sandy causes damage along the Connecticut shore.

1873 — **1917** — **1941–1945** — **2012**

1873
Hartford becomes the sole capital of Connecticut.

1941–1945
Aircraft and boats built in Connecticut play a big role in World War II.

31

The number of women working at factories such as the Vought-Sikorsky plant in Stratford increased greatly during World War II.

Modern Connecticut

Into the 20th century, Connecticut remained a major manufacturing center. During World War II (1939–1945), workers made thousands of warplane engines. In 1954, the state produced the world's first **nuclear** submarine for the U.S. Navy. Connecticut also became famous for its insurance companies. Today, many **financial** companies are located in southwest Connecticut. Businesses are attracted by the number of well-educated, skilled workers in Connecticut, as well as the state's nearness to New York City.

Mark Twain

Samuel Clemens (1835–1910) was a famous author who wrote under the pen name Mark Twain. He moved to Connecticut in 1871 and built what he called his dream home in Hartford. There, he wrote his best-known books, including *The Adventures of Huckleberry Finn*. Twain was also interested in inventions. He spent money trying to make and sell products such as a printing machine. But Twain lost a fortune. This forced him to leave Hartford in 1891 and find a cheaper place to live. He never returned to his dream home. Today, the Mark Twain House is a popular tourist spot.

Opened in 1844, Hartford's Wadsworth Atheneum is the oldest continuously operating art museum in the country.

CHAPTER 4

Culture

Connecticut is a great place to experience a wide range of art and culture. From filmmakers to writers, artists of all kinds are attracted to the state's natural beauty. They can live peacefully in Connecticut and still be close to major art centers in cities such as New York and Boston. As a result, the works created by Connecticut's residents are enjoyed around the world.

Sports and Recreation

Outdoor activities are a big part of Connecticut's culture. People hike and camp in the state's woods. Along the shore, they can fish and sail.

Connecticut has no major professional sports teams. But fans still turn out to watch team sports. Basketball is particularly popular, thanks to the success of the University of Connecticut's basketball teams. The women's team set a record in 2016 with its 11th national championship victory—more than any other women's team ever.

University of Connecticut player Moriah Jefferson passes by an opponent during a game.

Connecticut has an official state folk dance. It's the square dance.

People who attend the annual Sailfest in New London can enjoy fireworks displays.

Festivals for Fun

Towns across Connecticut host festivals throughout the year. Each December 31, Hartford welcomes the new year with First Night. At this event, families bundle up to enjoy art and music across the city. The night ends with fireworks. Other towns hold fairs that honor their agricultural roots and the farming that still goes on today. For example, the yearly fair held in Brooklyn is more than 200 years old!

Resorts run by Connecticut's Native Americans have a range of facilities, from stores and restaurants to spas and sports arenas.

Making a Living

Compared to the past, only a small number of Connecticut residents make their living in farming today. Manufacturing has also shrunk over the years, though the state still makes submarines and other important products for the military. Most Connecticut residents work in service industries. These include everything from banking and insurance to government and health care. Tourism is also important in Connecticut. Many people visit **resorts** run by the Mohegans and Mashantucket Pequots.

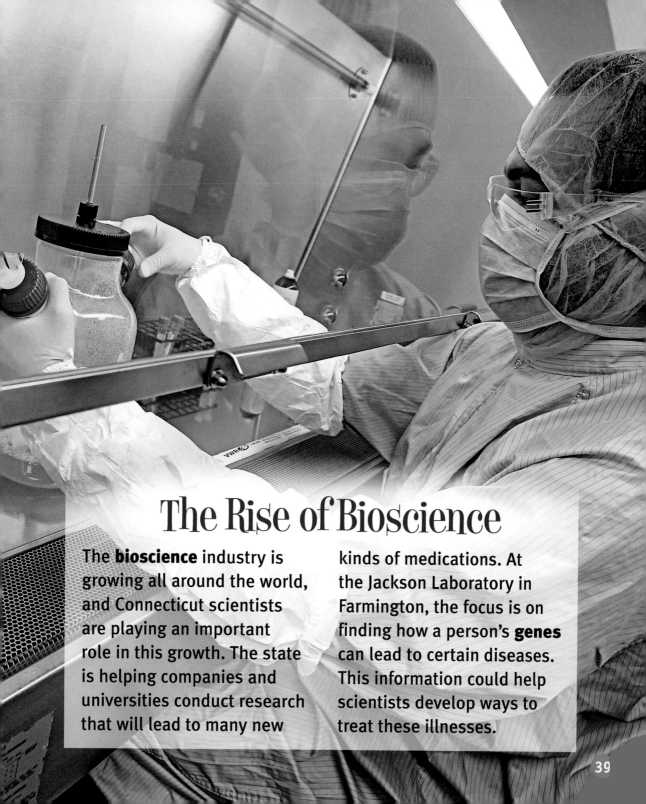

The Rise of Bioscience

The **bioscience** industry is growing all around the world, and Connecticut scientists are playing an important role in this growth. The state is helping companies and universities conduct research that will lead to many new kinds of medications. At the Jackson Laboratory in Farmington, the focus is on finding how a person's **genes** can lead to certain diseases. This information could help scientists develop ways to treat these illnesses.

Fabulous Food

Connecticut residents enjoy fruits, vegetables, milk, and eggs from local farms and shellfish from Long Island Sound. Immigrants brought with them foods such as Polish pierogies and Middle Eastern falafel. New Haven is famous for its pizza, and many people believe hamburgers were invented there.

  ## Blueberry Cobbler

Ask an adult to help you!

Blueberry patches are found across Connecticut, but you can also use other berries or fruit for this easy dessert.

Ingredients

3 cups fresh blueberries
1/2 cup plus 3 tablespoons sugar
1/3 cup orange juice
2/3 cup all-purpose flour

1/4 teaspoon baking powder
1 pinch salt
1/2 cup butter, softened
1 egg
1 teaspoon vanilla extract

Directions

Preheat the oven to 375 degrees F. Mix the blueberries, 3 tablespoons sugar, and orange juice in a greased 8-inch square baking dish. In a small bowl, mix the flour, baking powder, and salt. In a large bowl, mix the butter and 1/2 cup sugar until it forms a smooth, light paste. Add the egg and vanilla extract to the butter mixture and mix well. Gradually add the flour mixture to the large bowl and stir until all the ingredients are combined. Drop the batter by tablespoon on top of the fruit mixture. Bake the cobbler for 35 to 40 minutes and enjoy!

Small but Important

Connecticut may not be a very large state, but it has played a huge role in America's history. Residents like that they can find natural beauty all around them while remaining close to major cities. People from all over the world have settled in Connecticut, bringing new ideas and energy with them. This remarkable state is sure to remain a great place to live, work, and play for many years to come! ★

Famous People

Venture Smith

(ca. 1730–1805) wrote one of the first books describing life as a slave in America. Smith won his freedom and bought land in Stonington.

Noah Webster

(1758–1843) wrote the first dictionary of English as it was spoken in the United States. His name still appears on one of the most popular dictionaries used today. He was born in West Hartford.

Prudence Crandall

(1803–1890) opened a private school for African American girls in Canterbury. At the time, few schools of this kind existed in the United States.

Nathan Hale

(1755–1776) was a spy for the Americans during the Revolutionary War. He was caught by the British and hanged. He was born in Coventry.

Harriet Beecher Stowe

(1811–1896) was born in Litchfield and for many years was Mark Twain's neighbor in Hartford. She became world famous in the 1850s for writing *Uncle Tom's Cabin*, a novel that addressed the cruelty of slavery.

Igor Sikorsky

(1889–1972) designed aircraft and invented the first practical helicopter. Sikorsky flew his helicopter for the first time in Stratford in 1939.

Madeleine L'Engle

(1918–2007) wrote the beloved children's book *A Wrinkle in Time*, along with several other novels. The farmhouse she owned in Goshen inspired the setting of her most famous book.

Marian Anderson

(1897–1993) was an opera singer who overcame racial discrimination to become one of the greatest singers of her time. She lived for several decades on a farm in Danbury.

Ella Grasso

(1919–1981) entered politics in the 1950s and was later elected Connecticut's governor. She was the first woman in the country to become governor without following her husband into office.

Paul Newman

(1925–2008) won fame as a Hollywood actor before moving to Westport. While living in Connecticut, he continued acting and raced cars. He also founded Newman's Own, a food company that donates the money it makes to charity.

George W. Bush

(1946–) was the 43rd president of the United States and the only president born in Connecticut. His family was living in New Haven at the time. His father, George H. W. Bush, also served as president.

Did You Know That . . .

P. T. Barnum won fame for starting a circus in 1871 that he called "The Greatest Show on Earth." His name was connected to the circus until it closed in 2017. Barnum also once served as the mayor of Bridgeport.

In 1901, Connecticut passed the first law setting speed limits for cars. The limit was 12 miles (19 kilometers) per hour in cities and 15 miles (24 km) per hour in the country.

The first telephone book was published in New Haven in 1878. Because few people owned phones at the time, the book listed only 15 people.

A New Haven company sold the first lollipops made in the United States. It also invented a machine to produce lollipops faster. These early lollipops sold for one cent each.

During the 1970s, scientists began to study people living in and near the town of Old Lyme who were suffering from an unknown disease. Its symptoms included rashes, fever, headaches, and fatigue. The scientists named the new illness Lyme disease, after the town.

Walter Camp is sometimes called the father of American football. As a student and coach at Yale University, he helped write the rules that made the American game distinct from rugby.

Did you find the truth?

T Many U.S. Navy submarines are made in Connecticut.

F Connecticut is the third-largest state in the country.

Resources

Books

Nonfiction

Cunningham, Kevin. *The Connecticut Colony*. New York: Children's Press, 2012.

Kent, Zachary. *Connecticut*. New York: Children's Press, 2014.

Fiction

Estes, Eleanor. *Ginger Pye*. New York: Harcourt Brace, 1951.

Lawson, Robert. *Rabbit Hill*. New York: Penguin Books, 1944.

Speare, Elizabeth George. *The Witch of Blackbird Pond*. Boston: Houghton Mifflin, 1958.

Twain, Mark. *A Connecticut Yankee in King Arthur's Court*. New York: Charles L. Webster & Co., 1889.

Visit this Scholastic website for more information on Connecticut:

★ www.factsfornow.scholastic.com
Enter the keyword **Connecticut**

Important Words

armory (AR-muh-ree) a place where guns are made or stored

bioscience (BYE-oh-sye-uhns) a type of science that studies living things and how they function

colonial (kuh-LOH-nee-uhl) related to a time in history when people from foreign countries came to North America and formed settlements

financial (fye-NAN-shuhl) relating to money and how it is spent to make more money

genes (JEENZ) groups of chemicals in living things that shape how they look and act

immigrants (IM-i-gruhntz) people who move from one country to settle in another

nuclear (NOO-klee-ur) using the energy from the nucleus, or center, of tiny particles in certain materials

Puritans (PYOOR-uh-tins) members of a religious group that aimed to change the traditions of the Church of England to make it more "pure"

resorts (rih-ZORTS) places where people go for rest and recreation

silt (SILT) sand or other fine particles of soil that are carried along by flowing water and eventually settle to the bottom of a river

Index

Page numbers in **bold** indicate illustrations.

About the Author

Michael Burgan has written more than 250 books for children. He was born and raised in Connecticut and earned a degree in history from the University of Connecticut. He now lives in New Mexico, but he visits friends and family in his home state every year.